T0057068

BOB CHILCOTT
A Little Jazz Piano

for solo piano

MUSIC DEPARTMENT

OXFORD
UNIVERSITY PRESS

for Becky and Ollie

A Little Jazz Piano

1. Bobbing along

BOB CHILCOTT

© Oxford University Press 2020

Printed in Great Britain

OXFORD UNIVERSITY PRESS, MUSIC DEPARTMENT, GREAT CLARENDON STREET, OXFORD OX2 6DP

The Moral Rights of the Composer have been asserted. Photocopying this copyright material is ILLEGAL.

12
15
18
21
25
rit.
mp
p

2. *Becky's Song*

BOB CHILCOTT

© Oxford University Press 2020. Photocopying this copyright material is ILLEGAL.

13
f
mf
poco rit.
a tempo
16
p dolce
19
22
mp
rit.
25
p

3. *Walking with Ollie*

BOB CHILCOTT

© Oxford University Press 2020. Photocopying this copyright material is ILLEGAL.

13
16
19
f
22
25
mp
p